Chasing Shadows

Desert Sand Dunes

Photography by **Leo Touchet**

Photographs of Desert Sand Dunes
in Venezuela and North America

Chasing Shadows
Desert Sand Dunes

Design: Leo Touchet

Type: Garamond

ISBN-13: 978-1-7324433-2-7

First Edition
August 2018

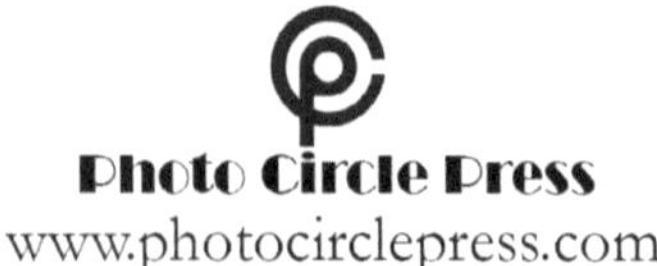

www.photocirclepress.com

To Elizabeth Burk

Chasing Shadows

Anita Pinedo Touchet, grew up near the Dunes of Coro on the Paraguaná Peninsula in western Venezuela. The dunes are known as Médanos de Coro National Park (*Parque Nacional Los Médanos de Coro*), and form the isthmus connecting the peninsula to the mainland. She told me stories of tourists riding camels in the sand dunes, and how she played there as a child.

In 1993, a corporate client sent me to Venezuela to photograph a petroleum refinery. By then, most of my photography work had transitioned from photojournalism to photographing for corporate publications and advertising. The assignment was to photograph the refinery on the Paraguaná Peninsula where Anita grew up. As I was preparing to leave for Venezuela, Anita asked me to take a few photographs of the sand dunes near Coro so she could have photos to show her friends.

After completing the assignment, on the highway back to Caracas, I came upon the dunes. I pulled over, grabbed my camera bag and headed into the dunes. The sun was about to set as I walked up into the dunes to a higher level. Suddenly, I found myself surrounded by sand and shadows which kept changing with every step. It then became a race with the setting sun, to photograph as much as possible before the dunes and shadows became darkness. It felt like I was chasing shadows.

For the following three years, I photographed as many dunes as possible. Photographs from the following dunes are included in this book:

The Dunes of Coro - Médanos de Coro National Park, Venezuela
Mesquite Flat Dunes - Death Valley National Park, California
Eureka Valley Sand Dunes - Death Valley National Park, California
Ibex Sand Dunes - Death Valley National Park, California
Tularosa Gypsum Dunes - White Sands National Monument, New Mexico
Monahans Sand Hills - Monahans Sandhills State Park, Texas
Big Dune - Amargosa Valley, Nevada

The Dunes of Coro - Médanos de Coro National Park, Venezuela

Médanos de Coro National Park (*Parque Nacional Los Médanos de Coro*) is a Venezuelan national park located in the state of Falcón_, near the city of Coro on the road that leads to Paraguaná Peninsula. The Peninsula is connected to the rest of the state by a natural isthmus of Médanos (sand dunes). The dunes cover approximately 54 square miles and some of the dunes are over 150 feet tall.

Mesquite Flat Dunes - Death Valley National Park, California

The Mesquite Flat Dunes are surrounded by mountains on all sides. Many of the Hollywood movies featuring dunes were filmed here due to their easy access by road. The largest dune (Star Dune) is between 130-140 feet tall. The dunes are composed of quartz and feldspar from the Cottonwood Mountains to the north.

Eureka Valley Sand Dunes - Death Valley National Park, California

The Eureka Valley Dunes are located in Inyo County, California. The dunes rise 680 feet from the valley floor and run parallel to the Last Chance Range in the southeastern tip of the Eureka Valley.

Ibex Sand Dunes - Death Valley National Park, California

The Ibex Dunes are located in the in the Mojave Desert, in San Bernardino County California in the southeastern corner of Death Valley National Park. The tallest dunes are over 150 feet about the valley floor. The dunes stretch more than two miles on the western side of the Saddle Peak Hills.

Tularosa Gypsum Dunes - White Sands National Monument, New Mexico

The Tularosa Gypsum Dunes cover 275 square miles of desert and preserves a piece of New Mexico's unique geology. The isolation and weather patterns of the Tularosa Basin create a truly unique experience. Typically, gypsum is rarely found as sand because it dissolves in contact with water.

Monahans Sand Hills - Monahans Sandhills State Park, Texas

The Monahans Sandhills are desert like, but are part of a semi-arid ecosystem which covers an area 70 miles long and 20 miles wide from Crane County, Texas to Andrews County, Texas. Some of the dunes are as tall as 70 feet. The state park is located near the town of Monahans.

Big Dune - Amargosa Valley, Nevada

Big Dune is located 100 miles northwest of Las Vegas. The dunes cover about five square miles. Big Dune is a 1.5 square mile complex star dune located at a base elevation of 2,435 feet and rises over 300 feet.. These dunes, are a recreational playground for off road vehicles. To view these dunes without tire tracks, one has start very early in the morning after a windy night.

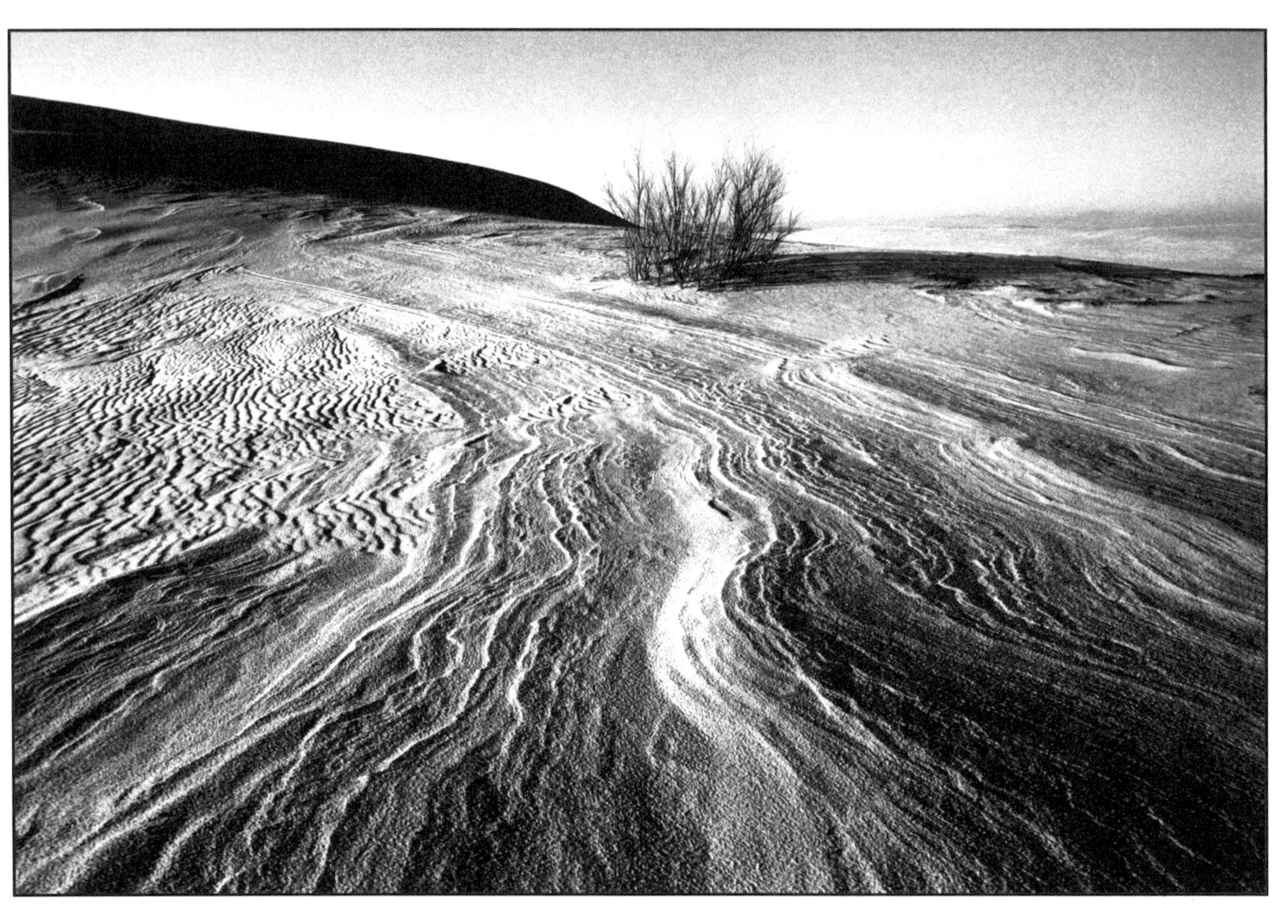

Tularosa Gypsum Dunes - White Sands National Monument, New Mexico 1994

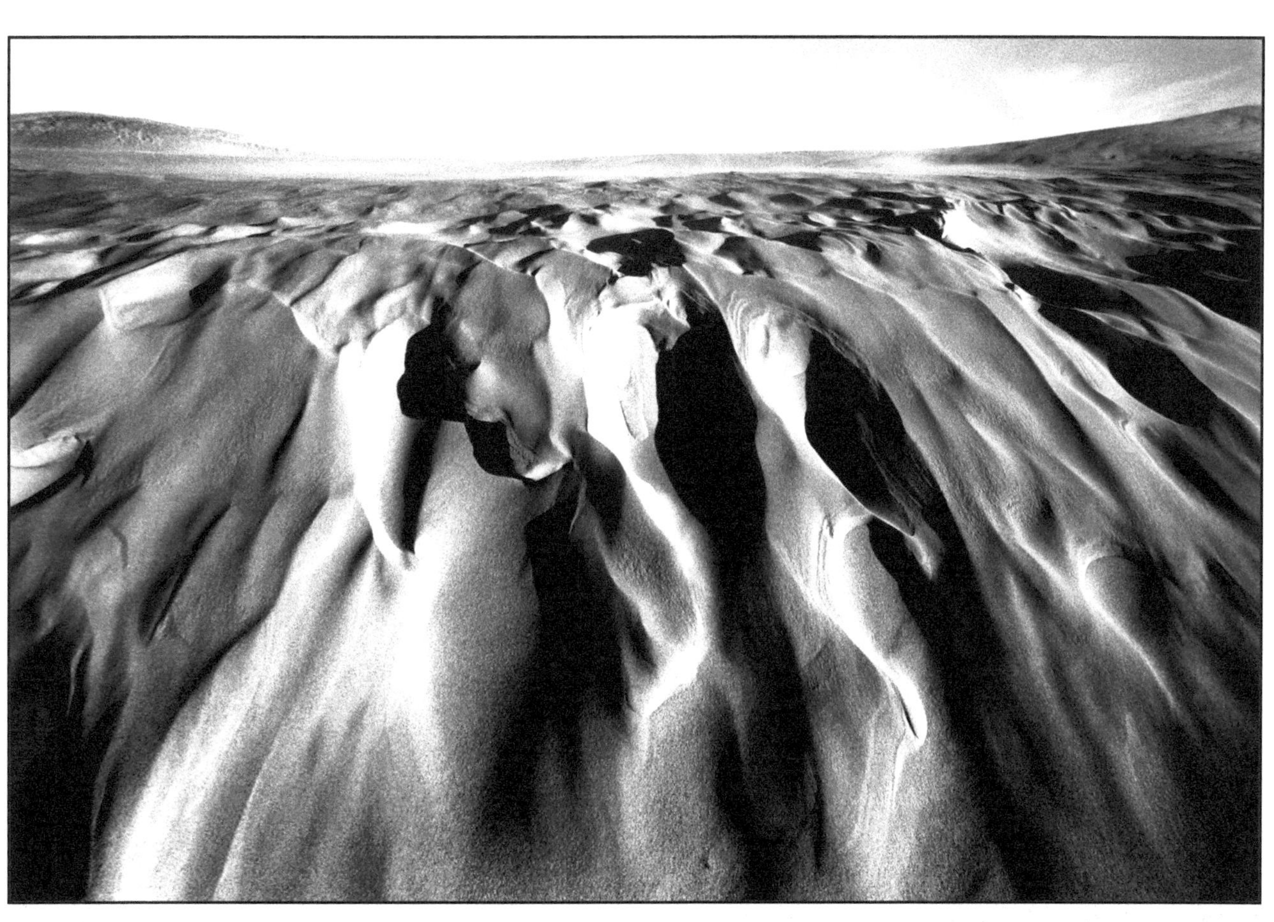

Monahans Sand Hills - Monahans State Park, Texas 1994

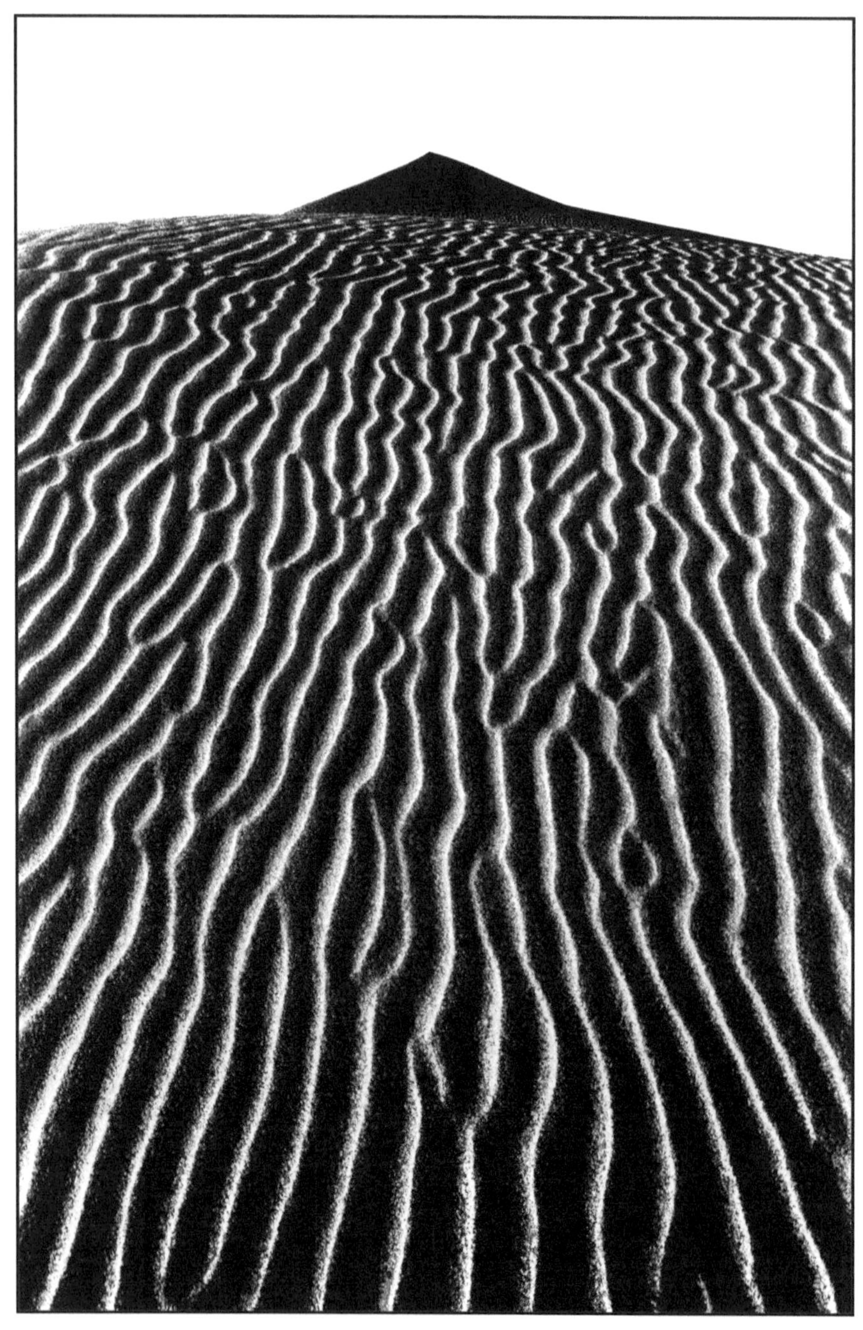

 Ibex Sand Dunes - Death Valley National Park, California 1996

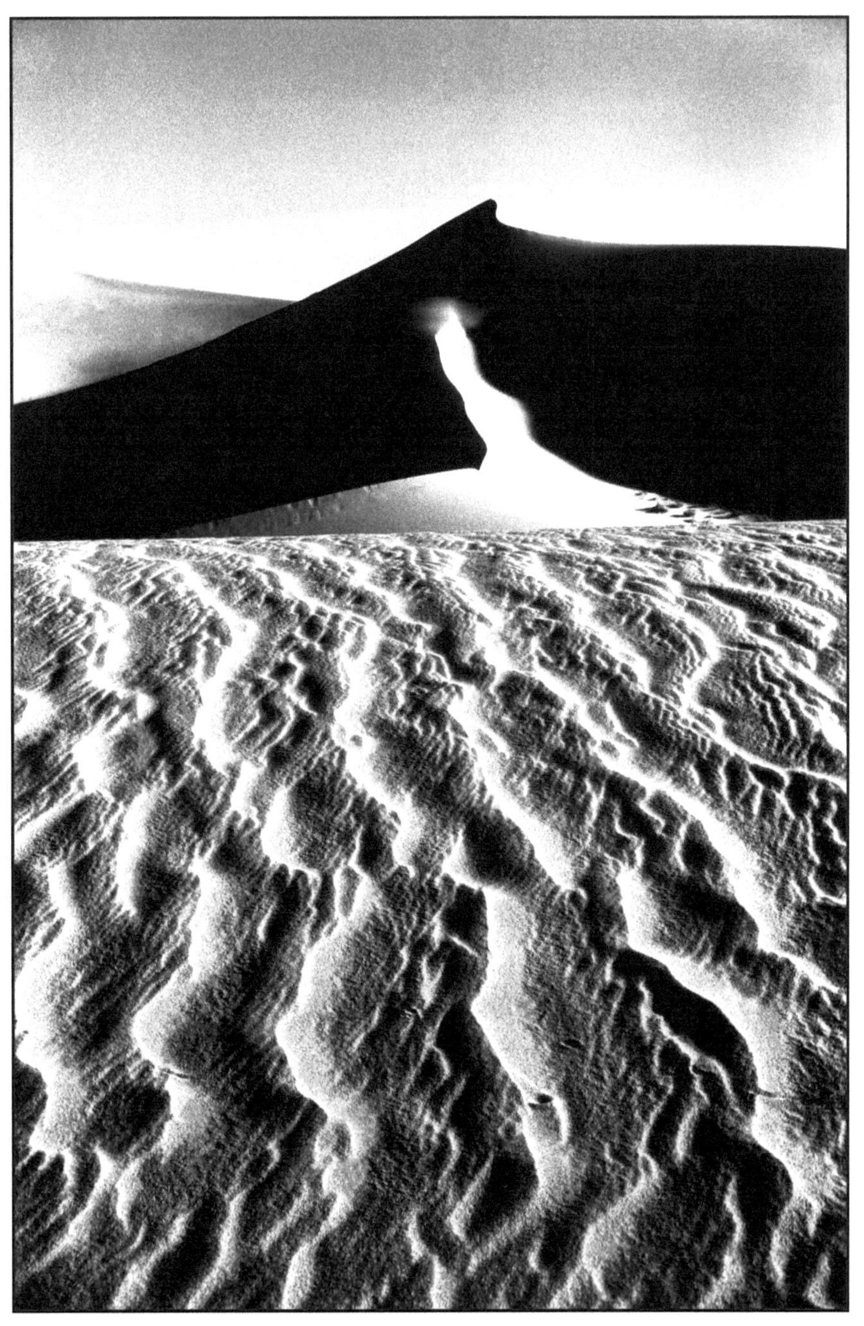

Eureka Valley Sand Dunes - Death Valley National Park, California 1996

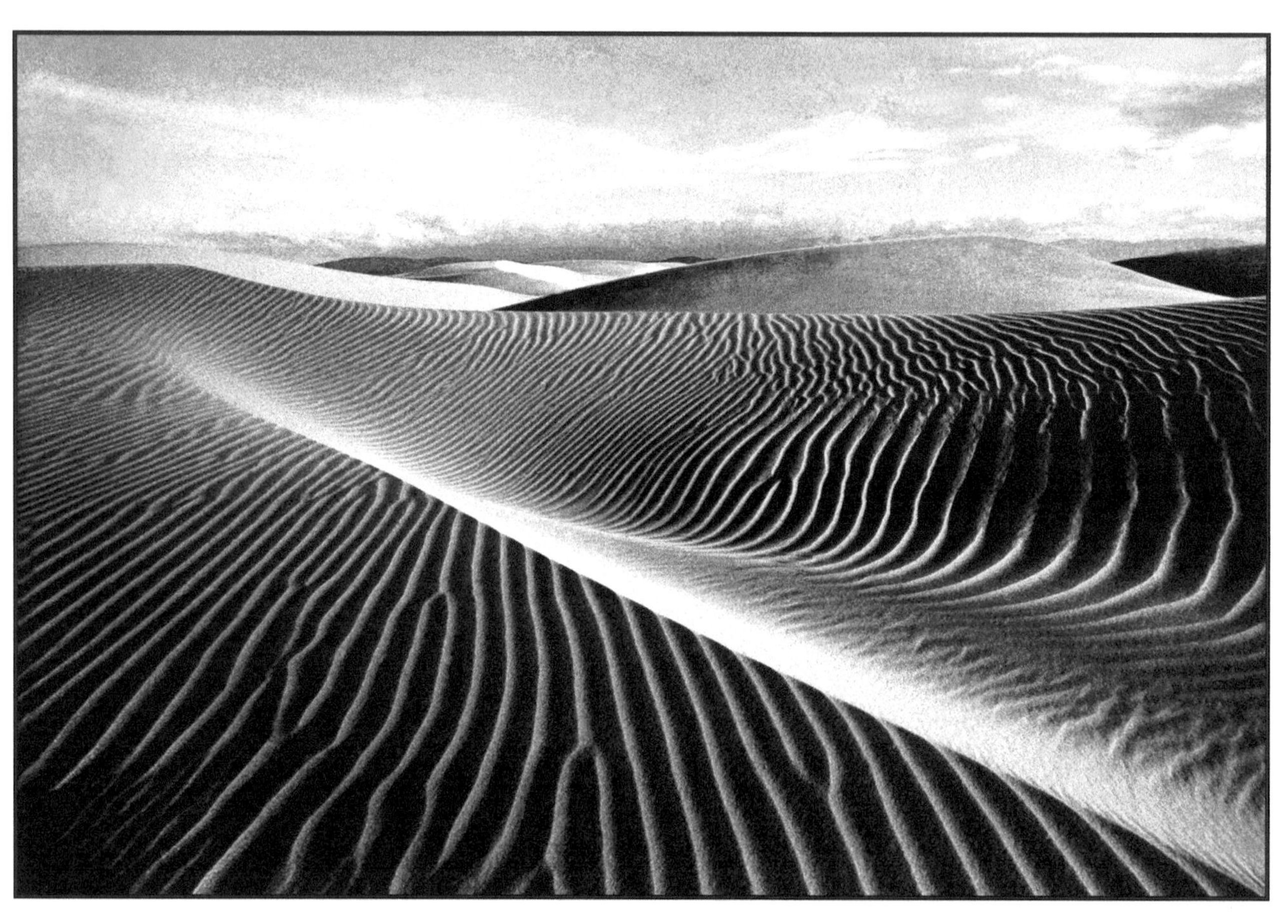

 Dunes of Coro - Médanos de Coro National Park, Venezuela 1993

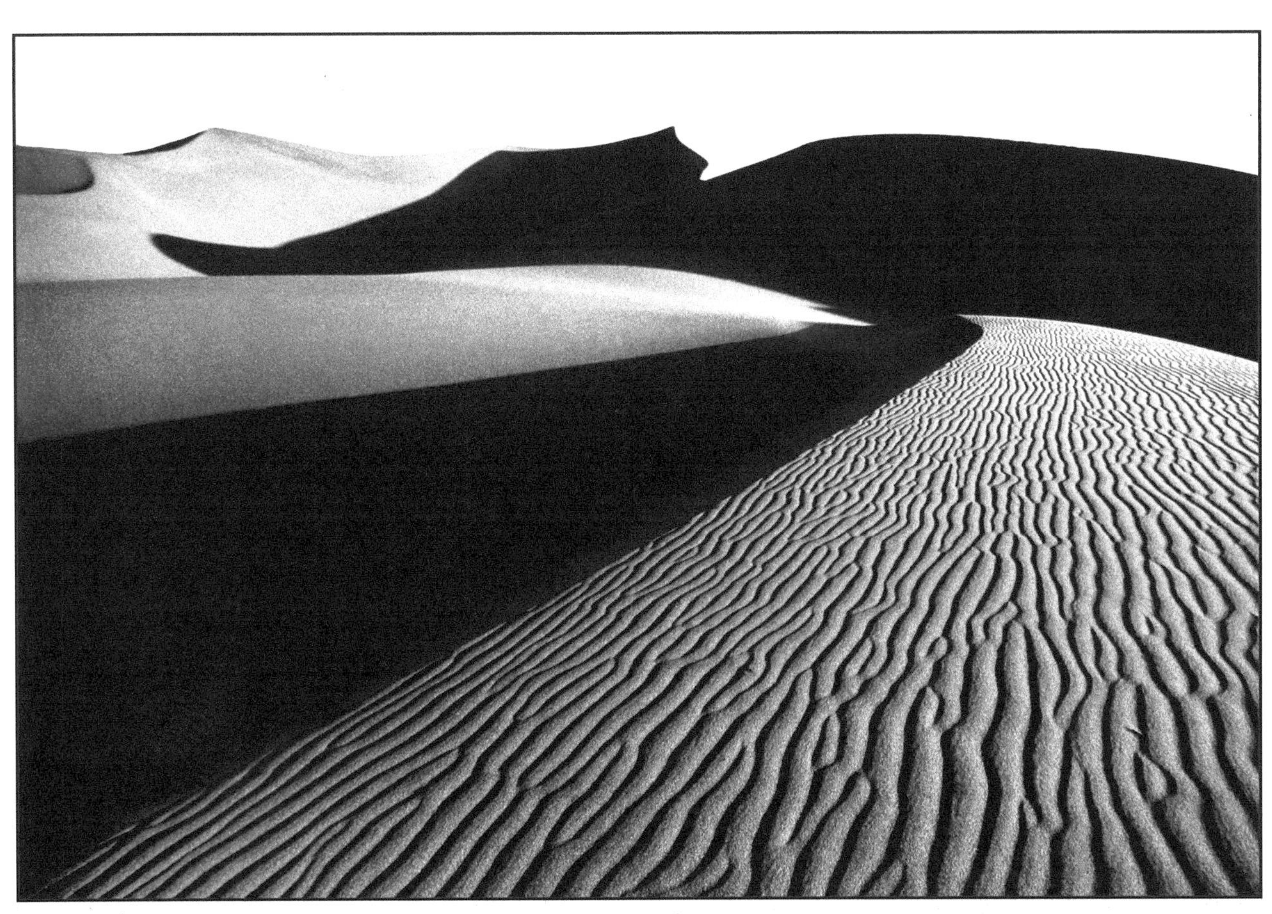

Eureka Valley Sand Dunes - Death Valley National Park, California 1996

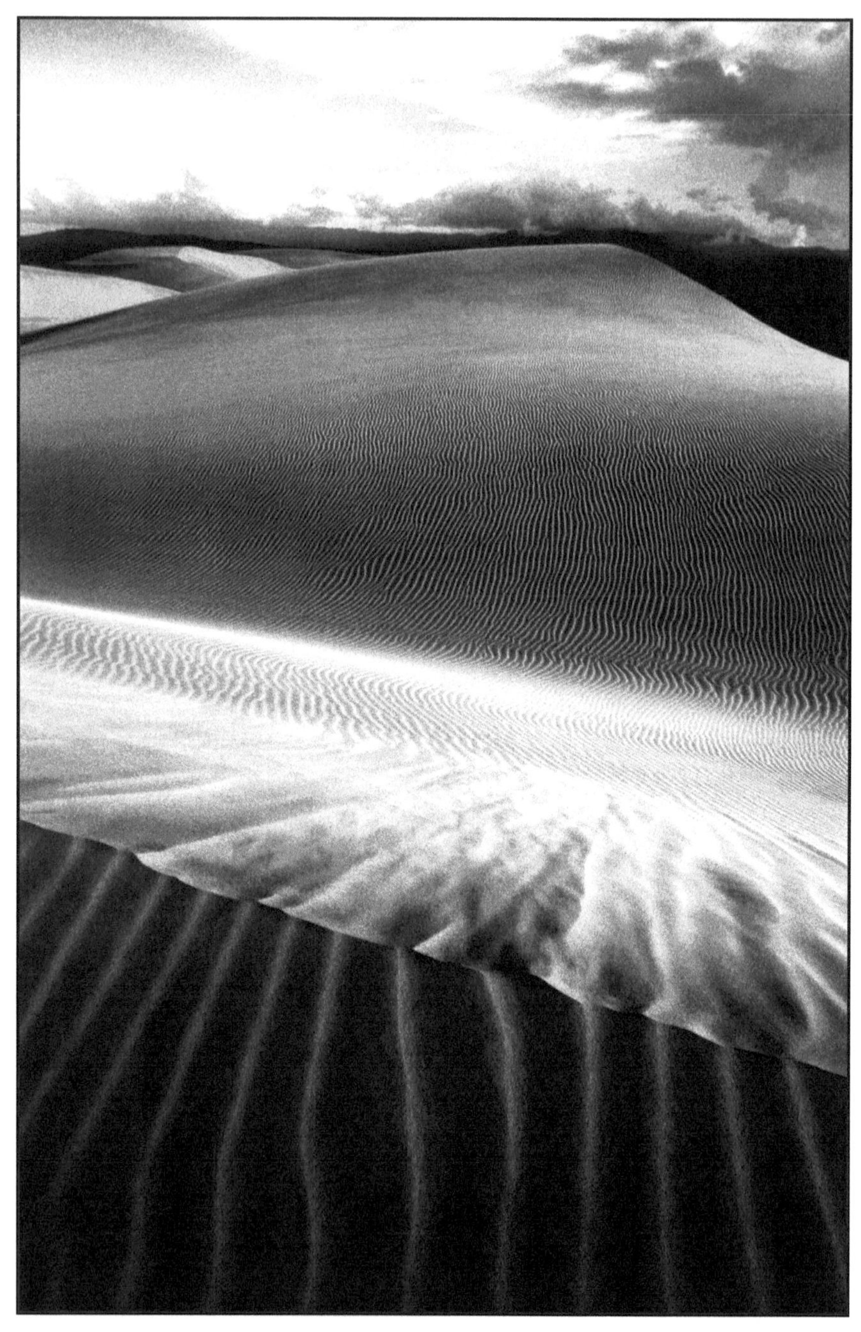

Dunes of Coro - Médanos de Coro National Park, Venezuela 1993

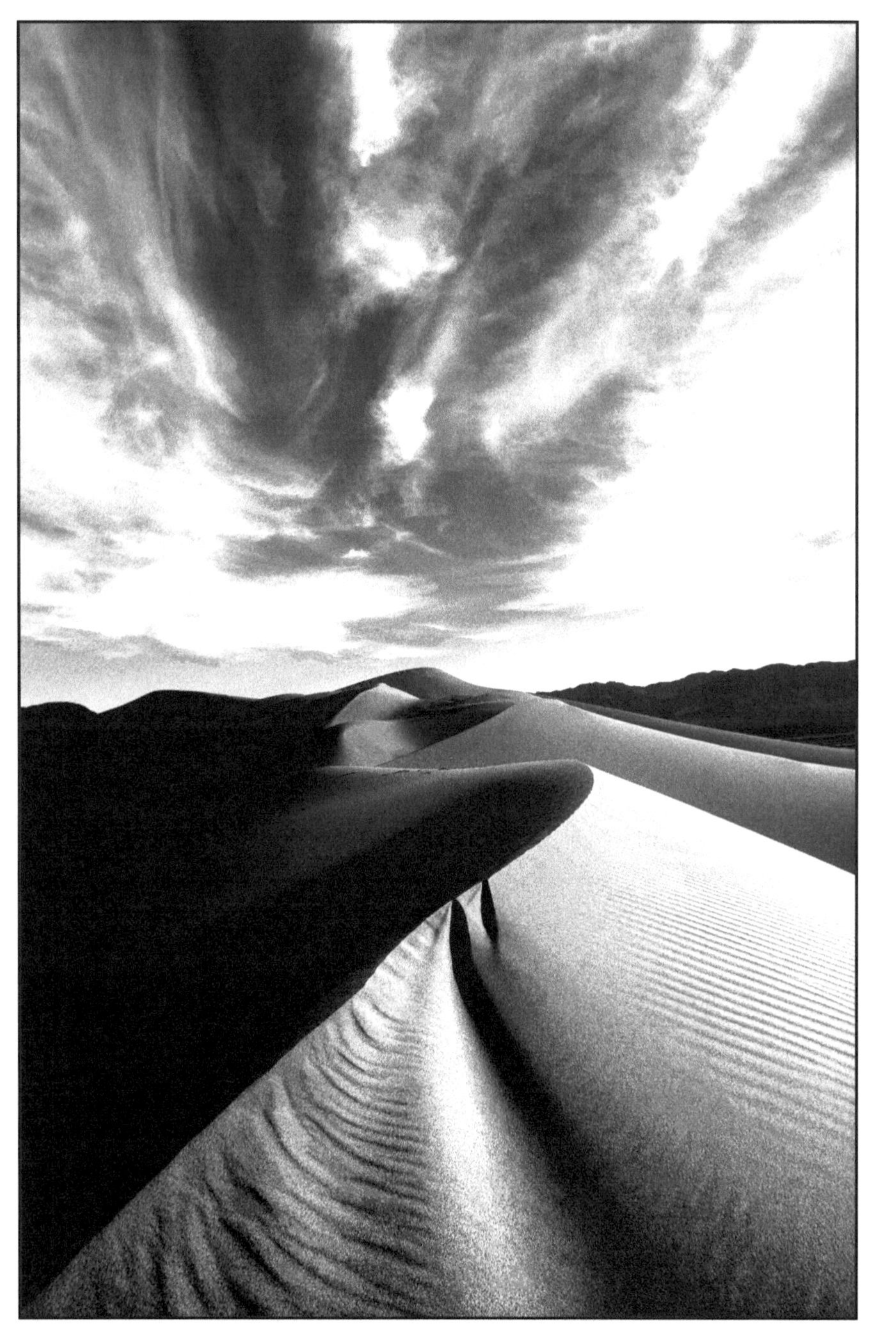

Ibex Sand Dunes - Death Valley National Park, California 1996

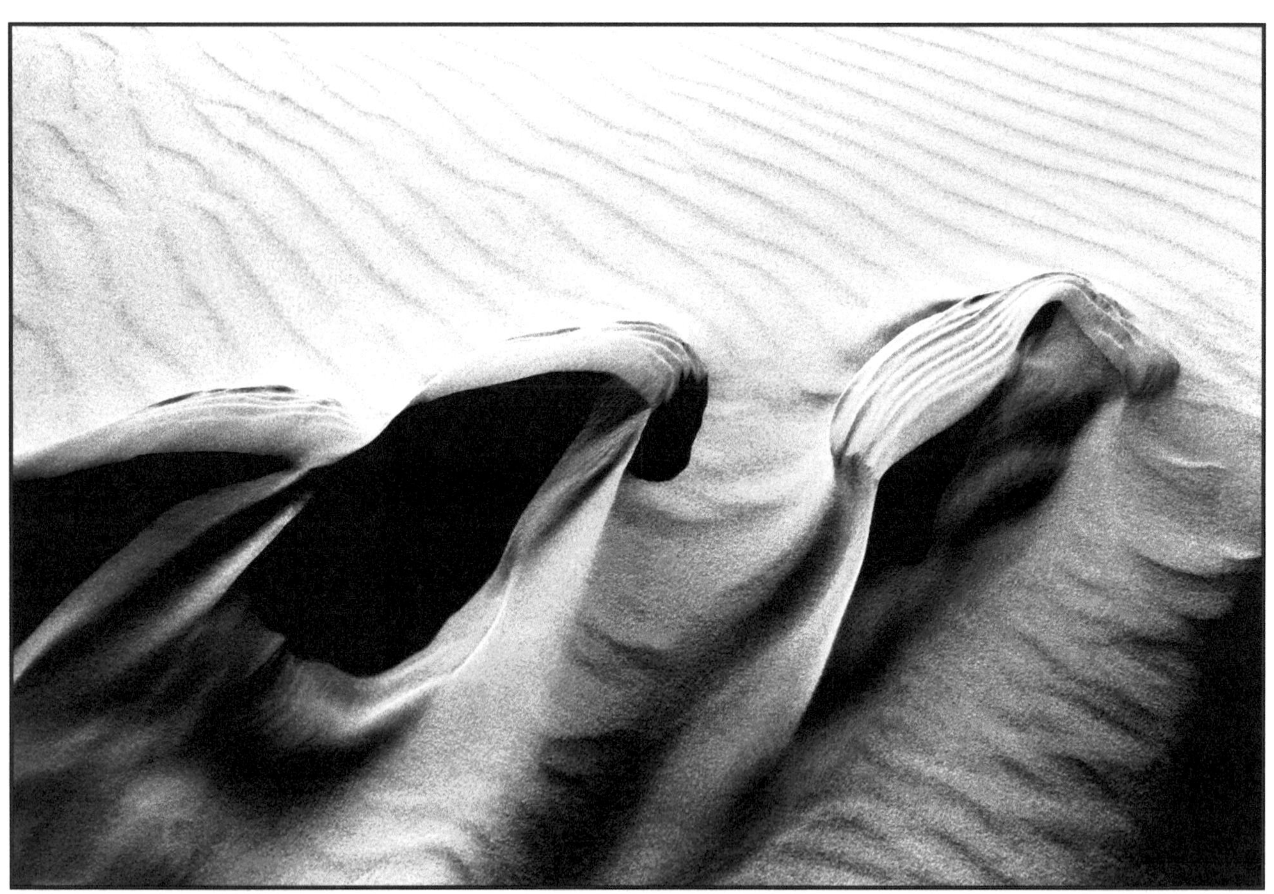

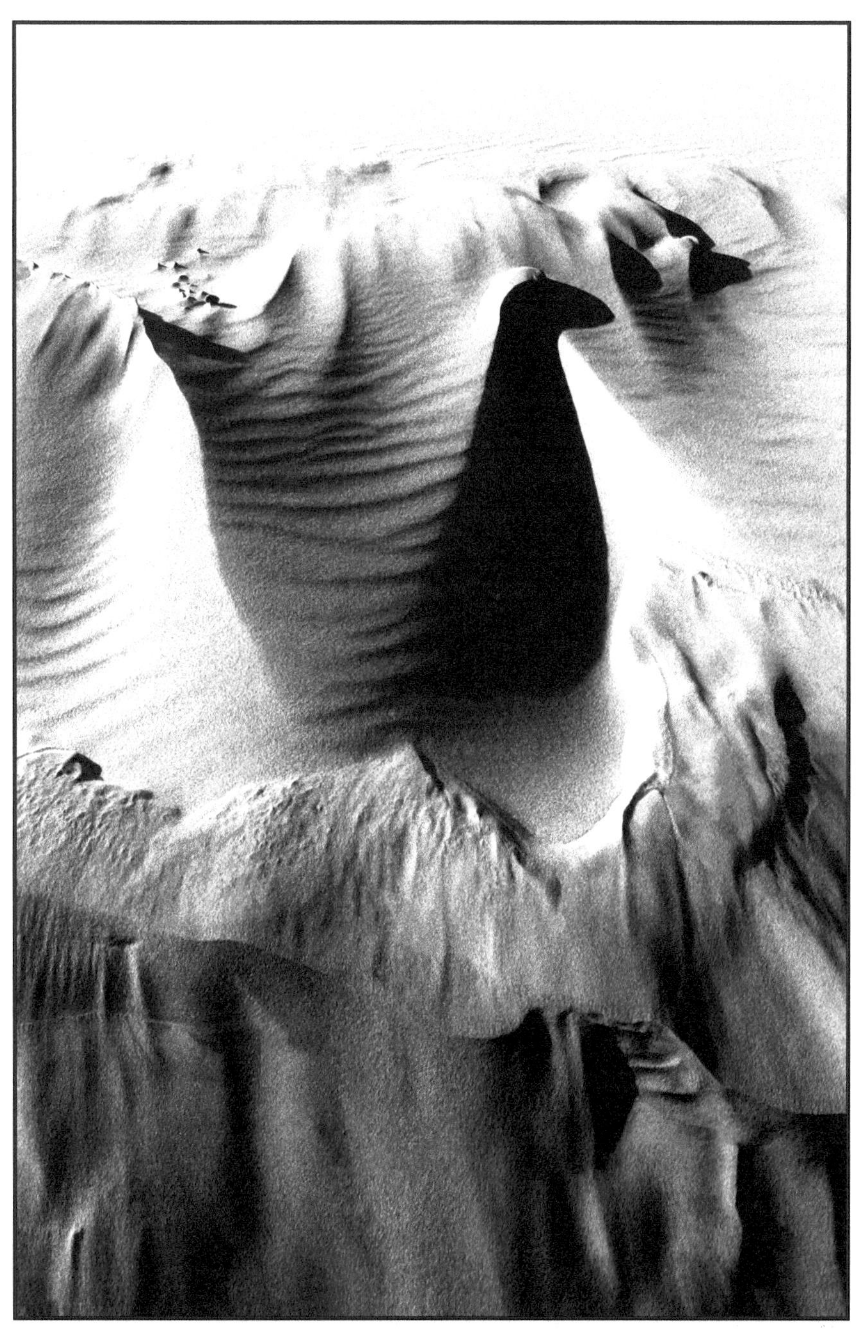

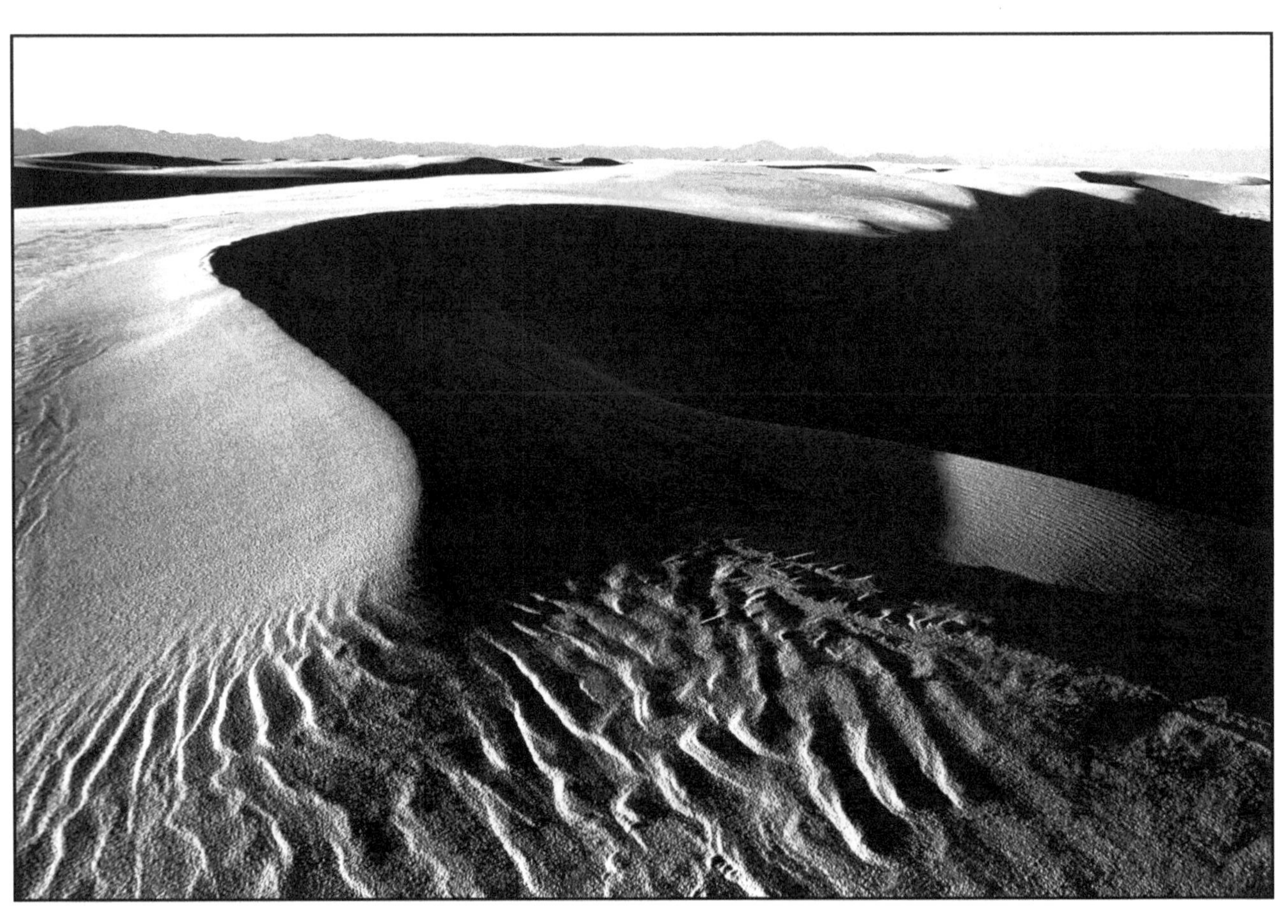

 Tularosa Gypsum Dunes - White Sands National Monument, New Mexico 1994

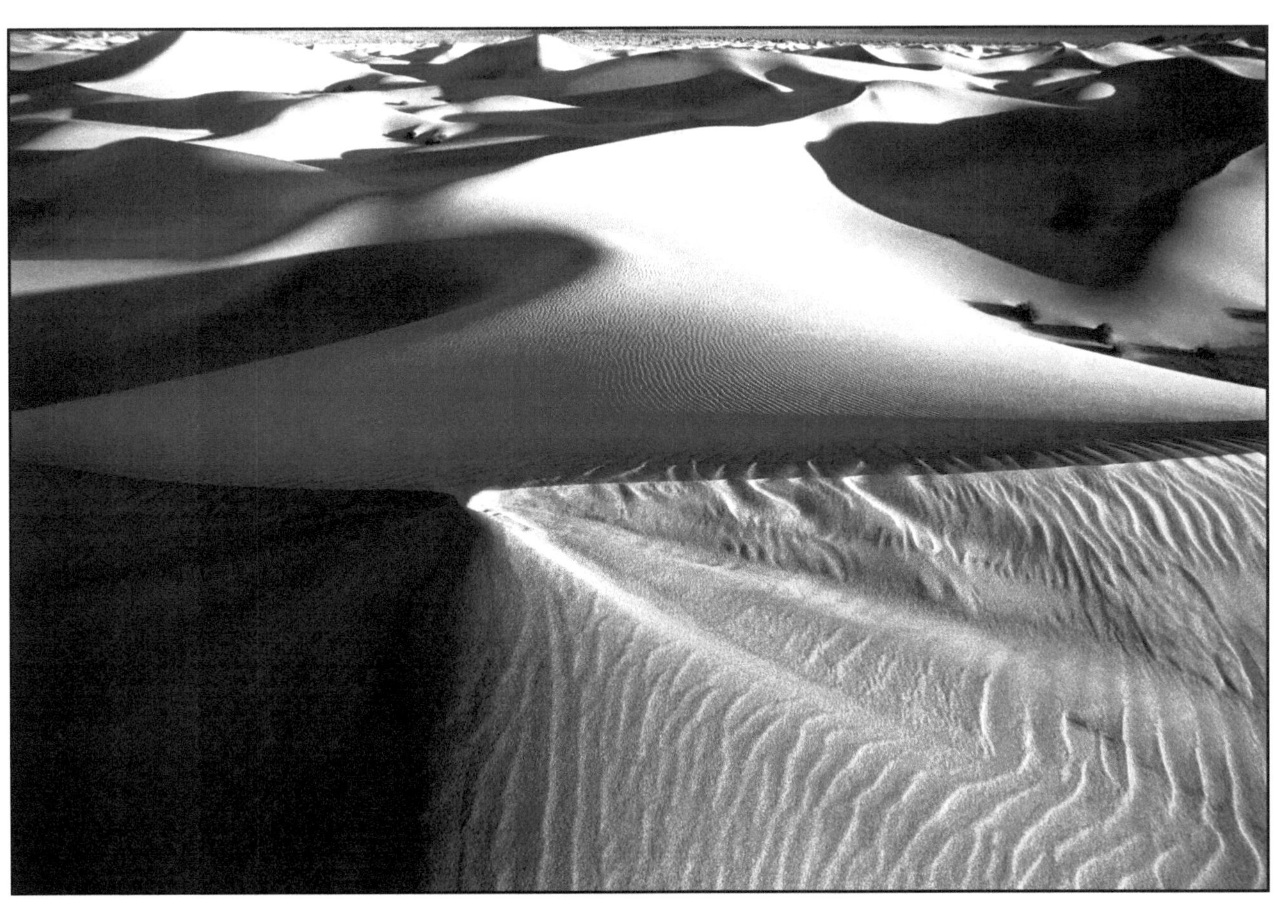

Mesquite Flat Dunes - Death Valley National Park, California 1996

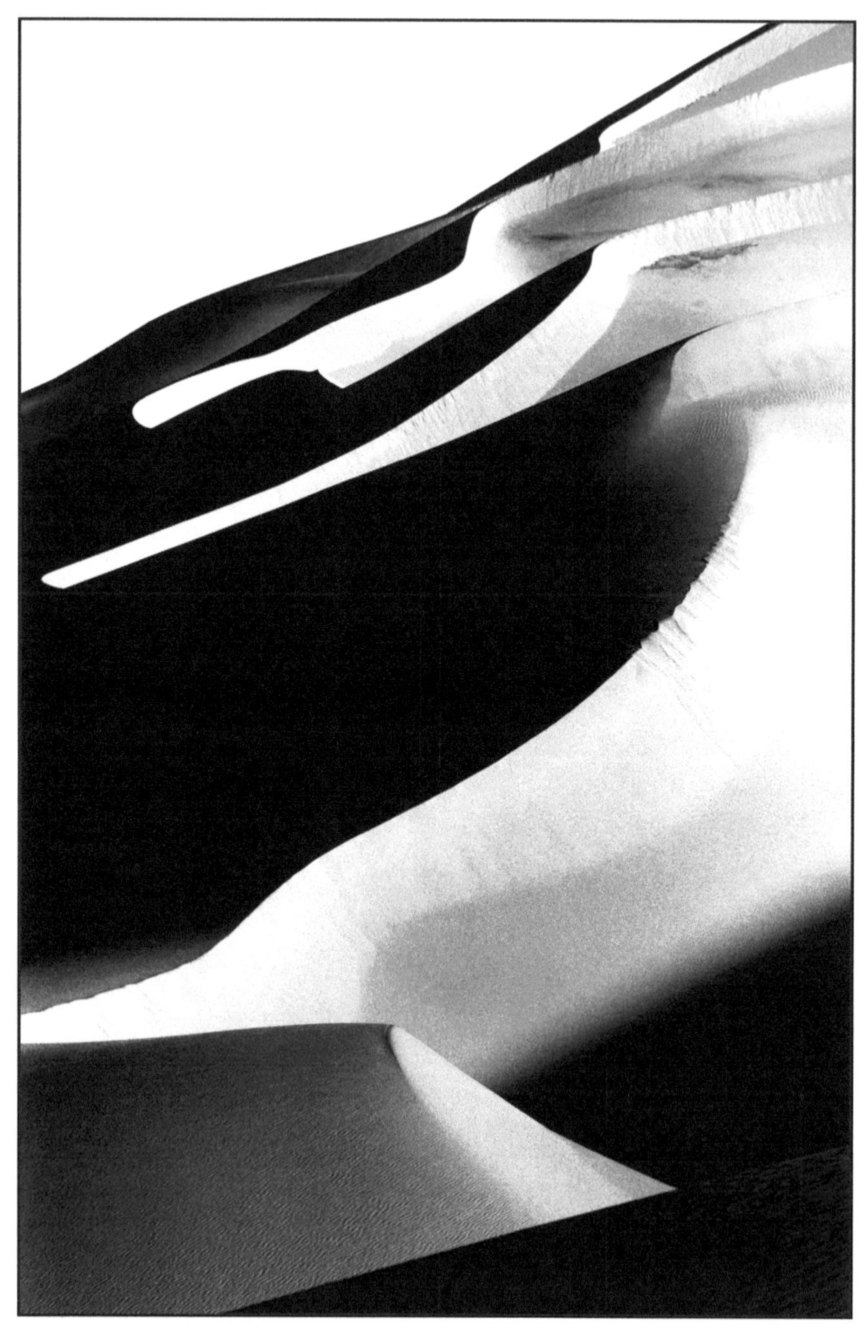

Eureka Valley Sand Dunes - Death Valley National Park, California 1996

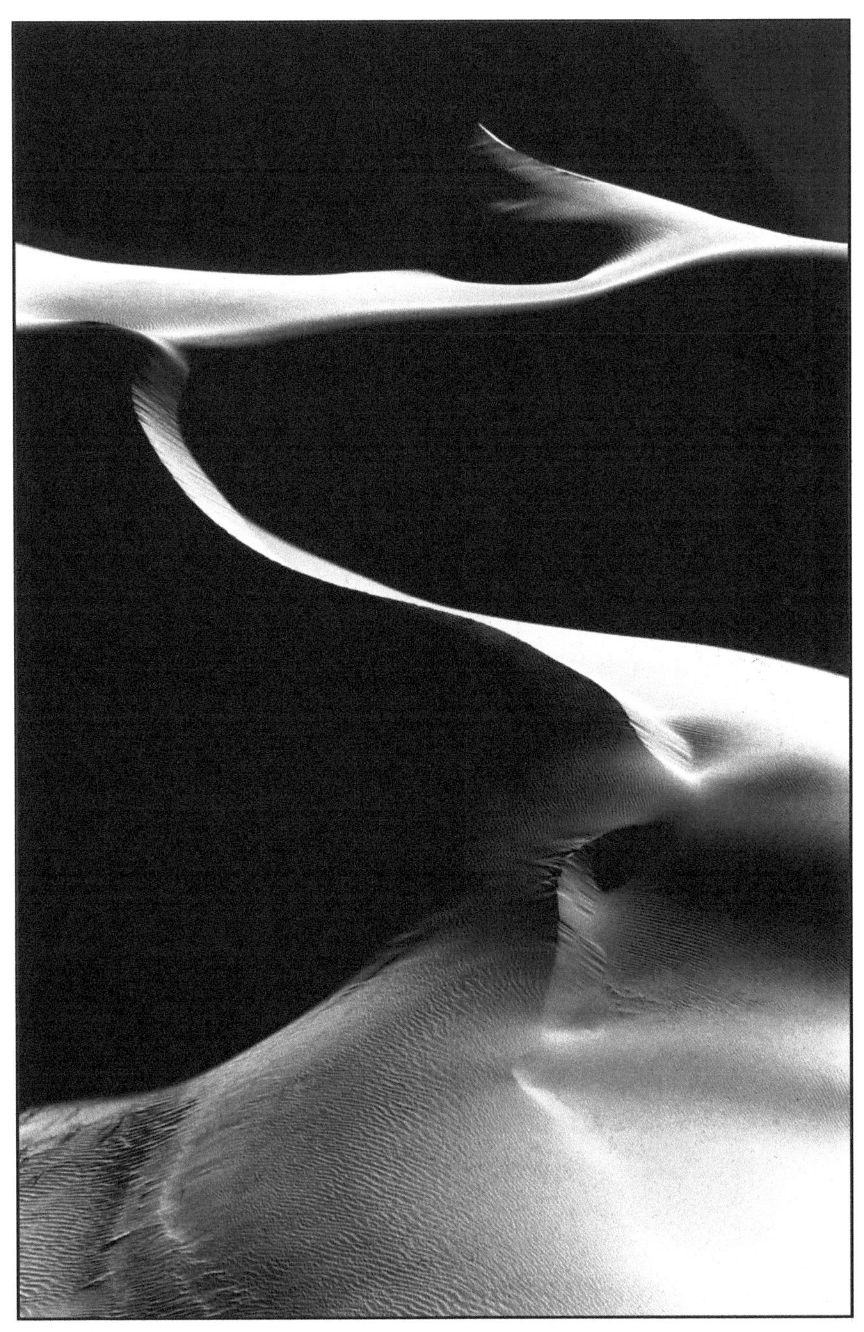

Eureka Valley Sand Dunes - Death Valley National Park, California 1996

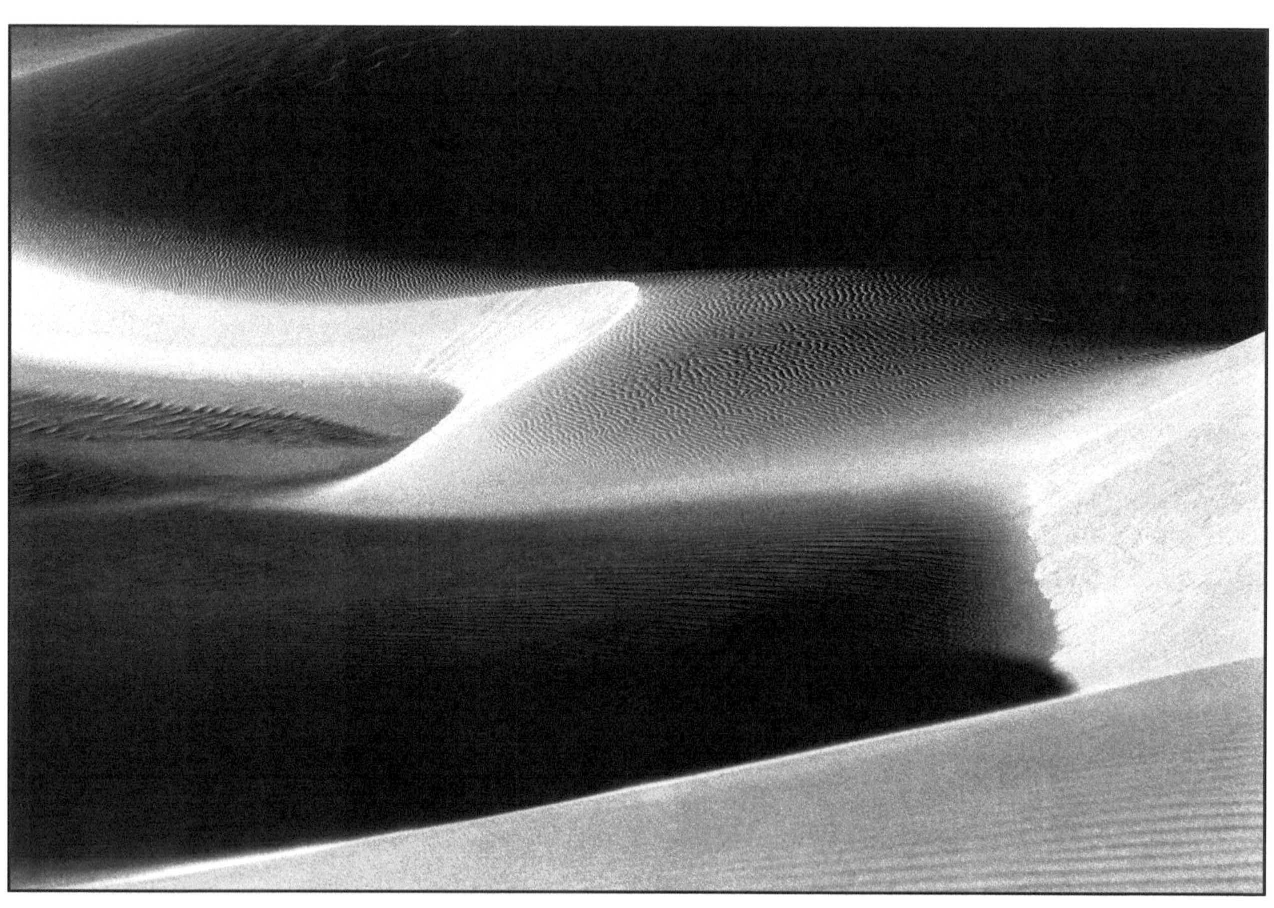

Big Dune - Amargosa Valley, Nevada 1996

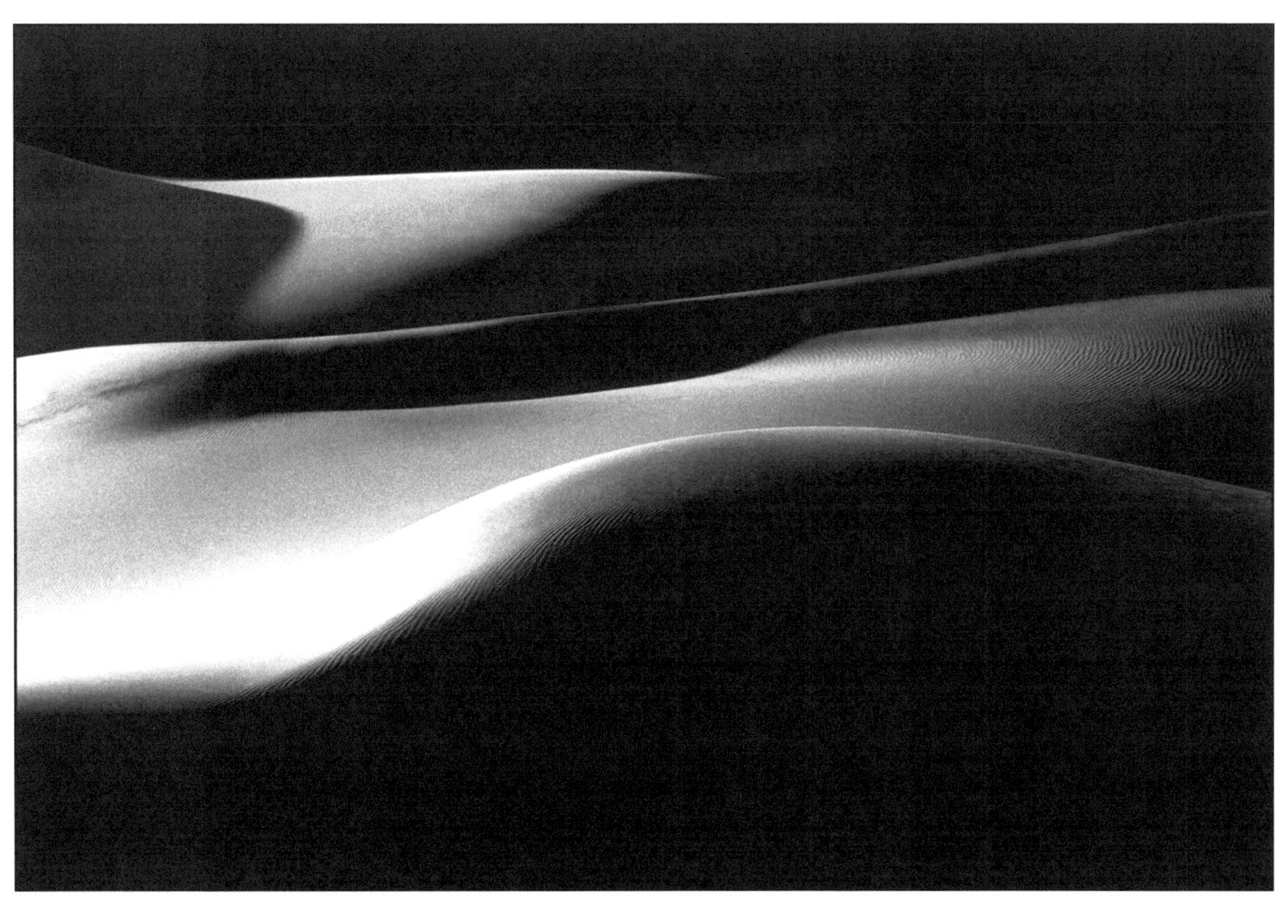

Mesquite Flat Dunes - Death Valley National Park, California 1996

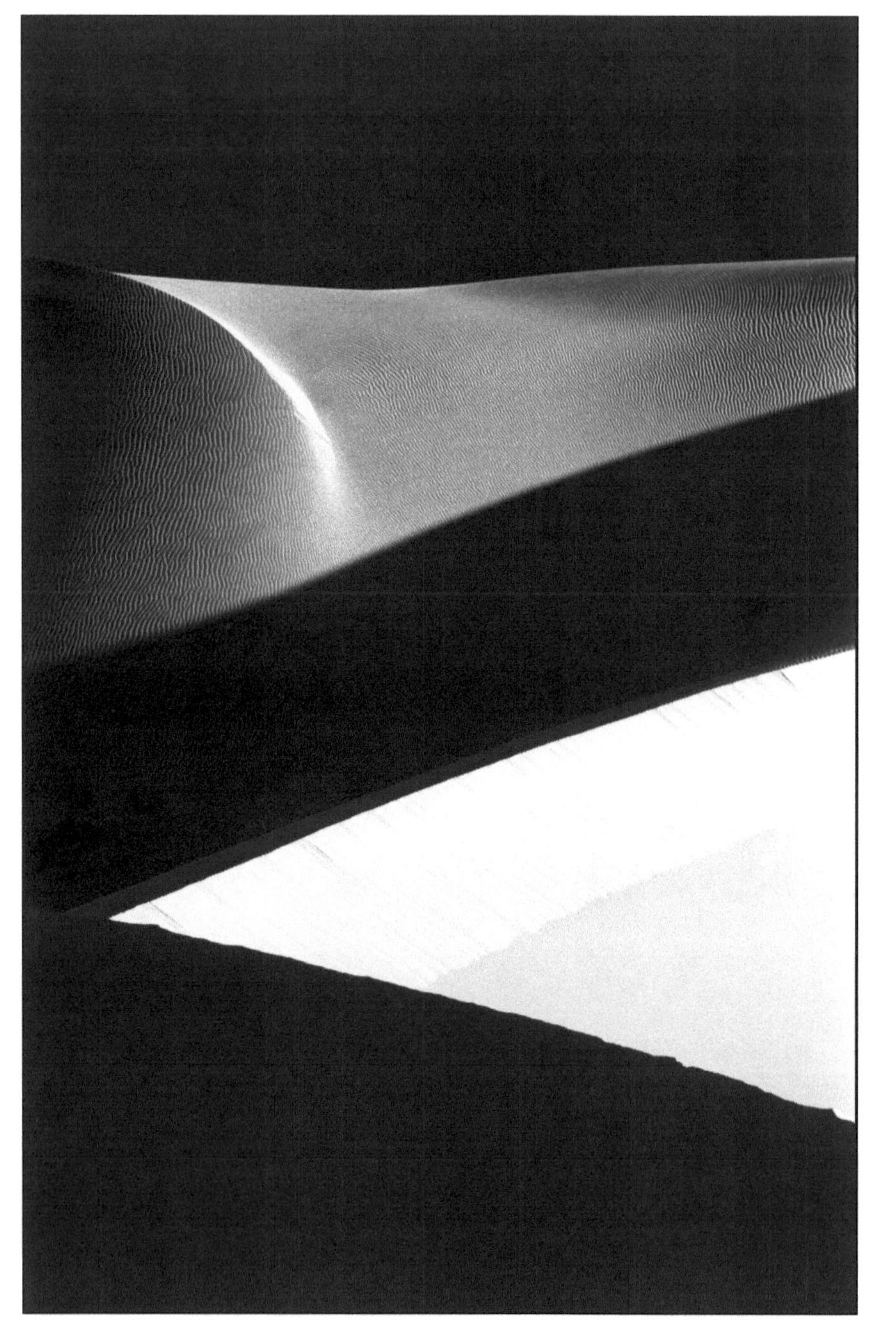

 Eureka Valley Sand Dunes - Death Valley National Park, California 1996

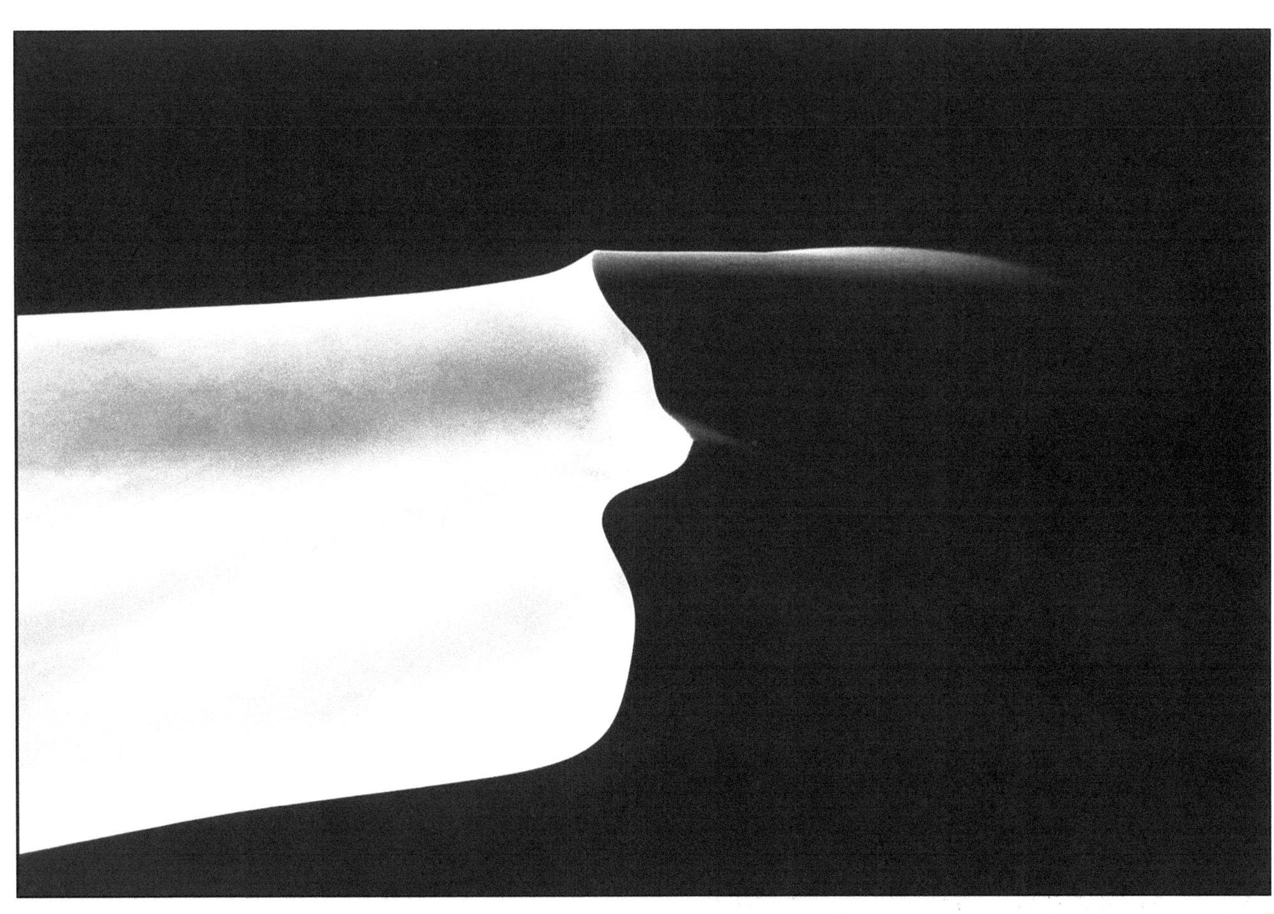

Eureka Valley Sand Dunes - Death Valley National Park, California 1996

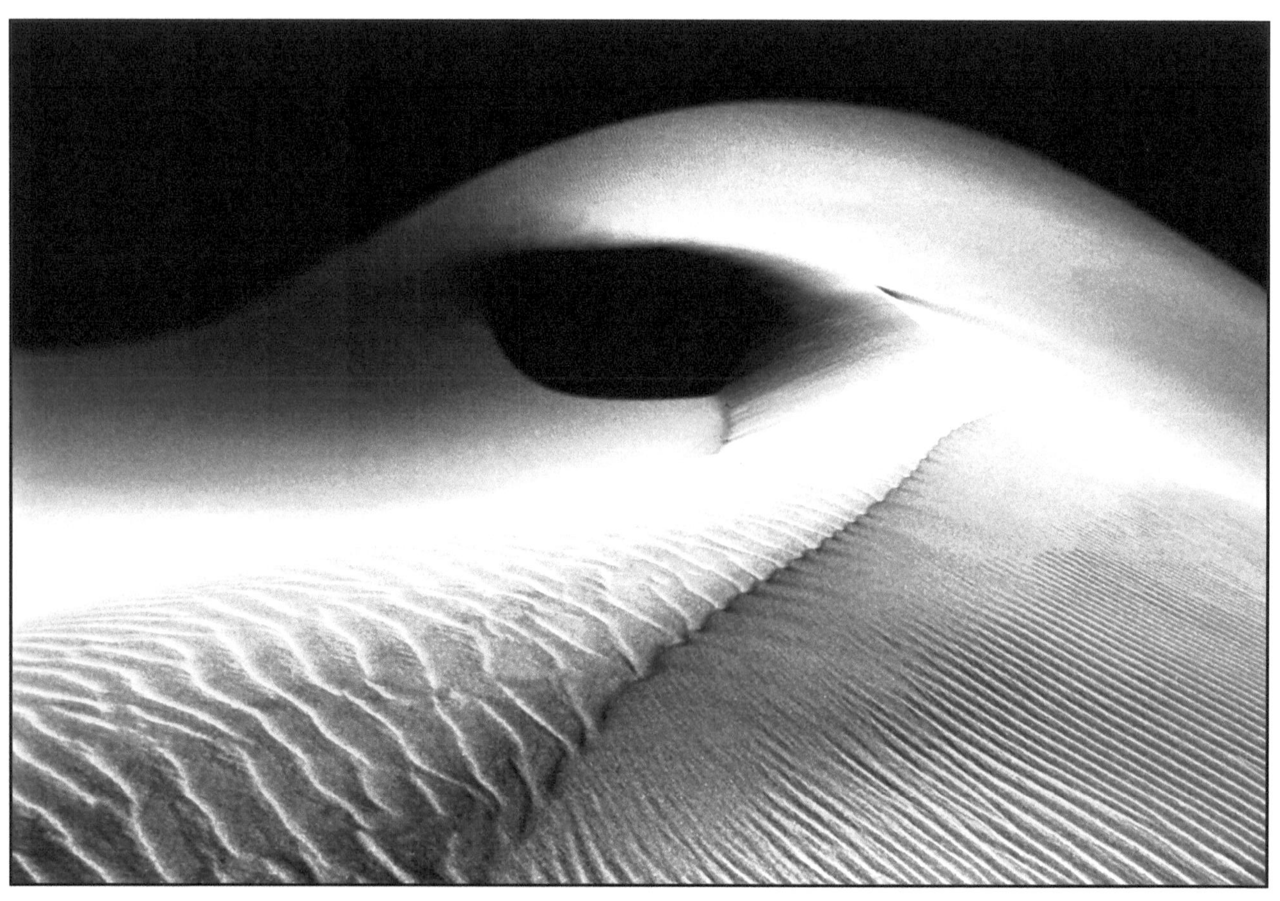

Eureka Valley Sand Dunes - Death Valley National Park, California 1996

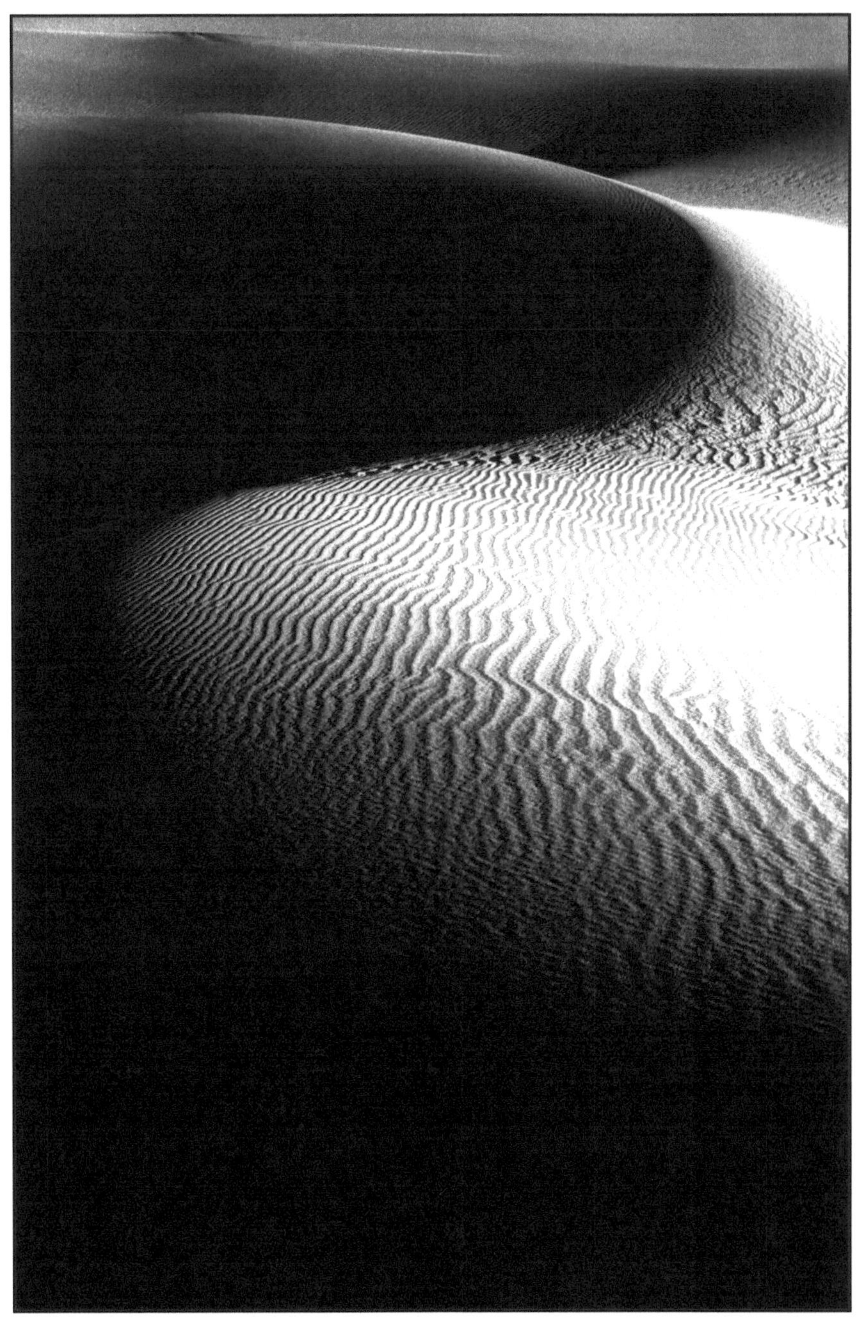

Mesquite Flat Dunes - Death Valley National Park, California 1996

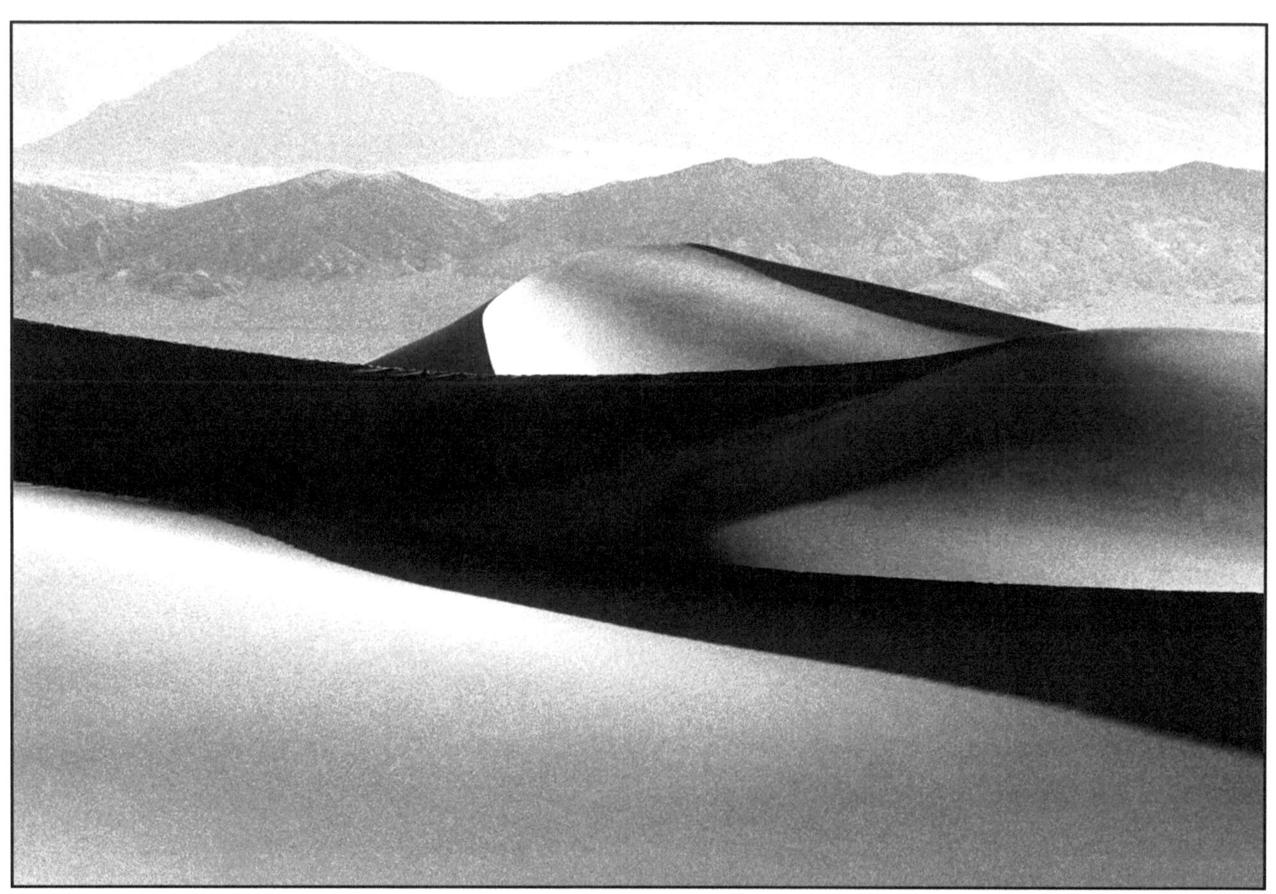

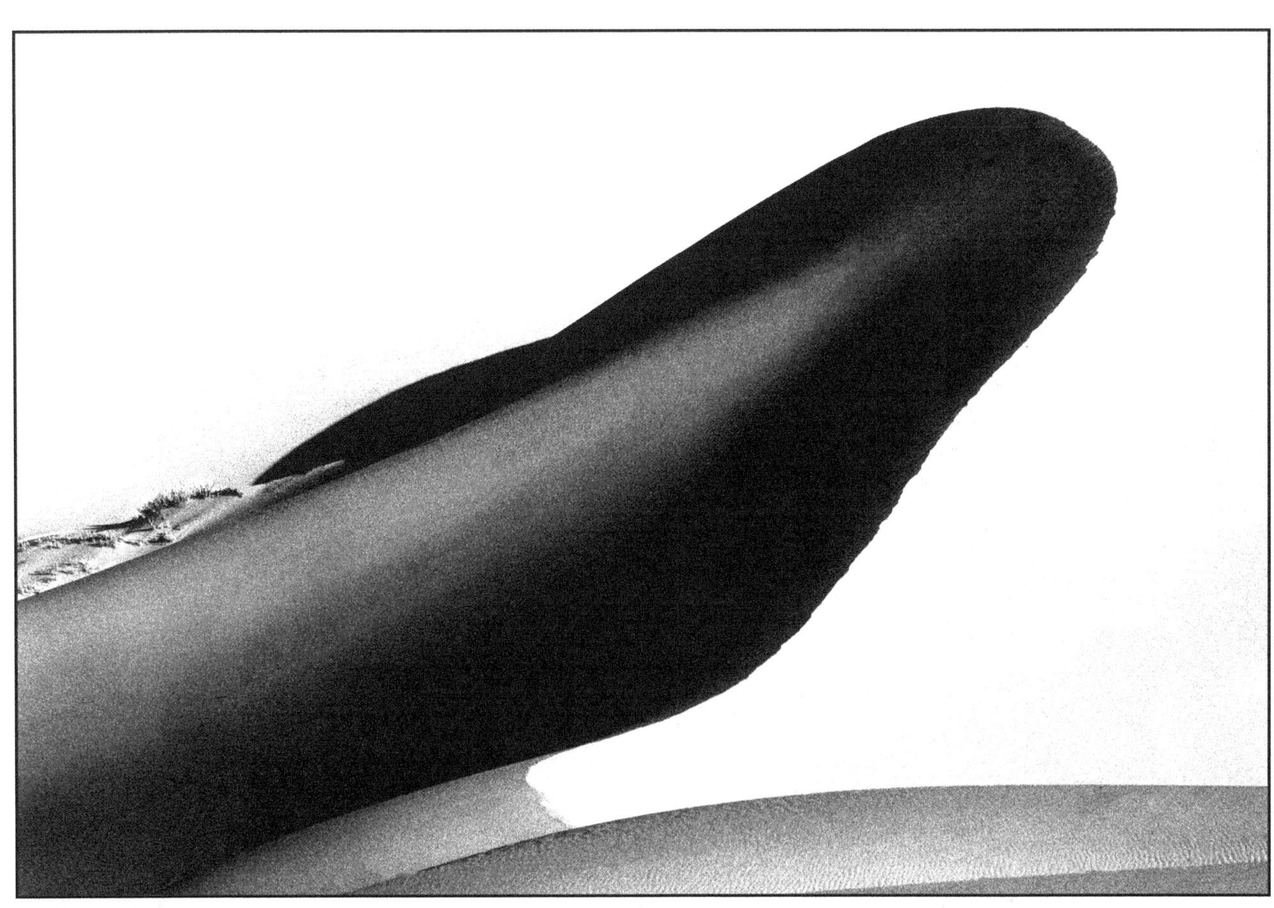

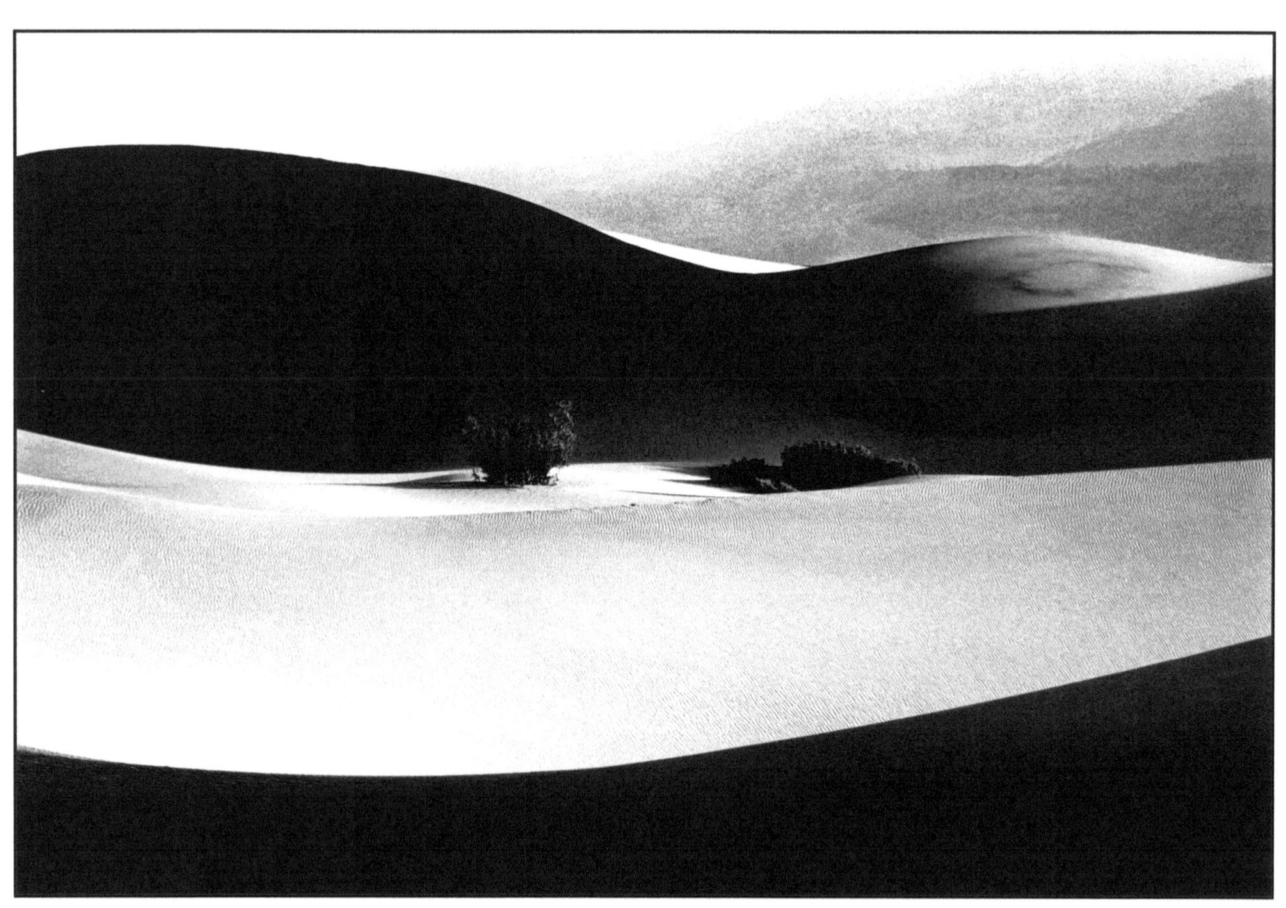

 Monahans Sand Hills - Monahans State Park, Texas 1994

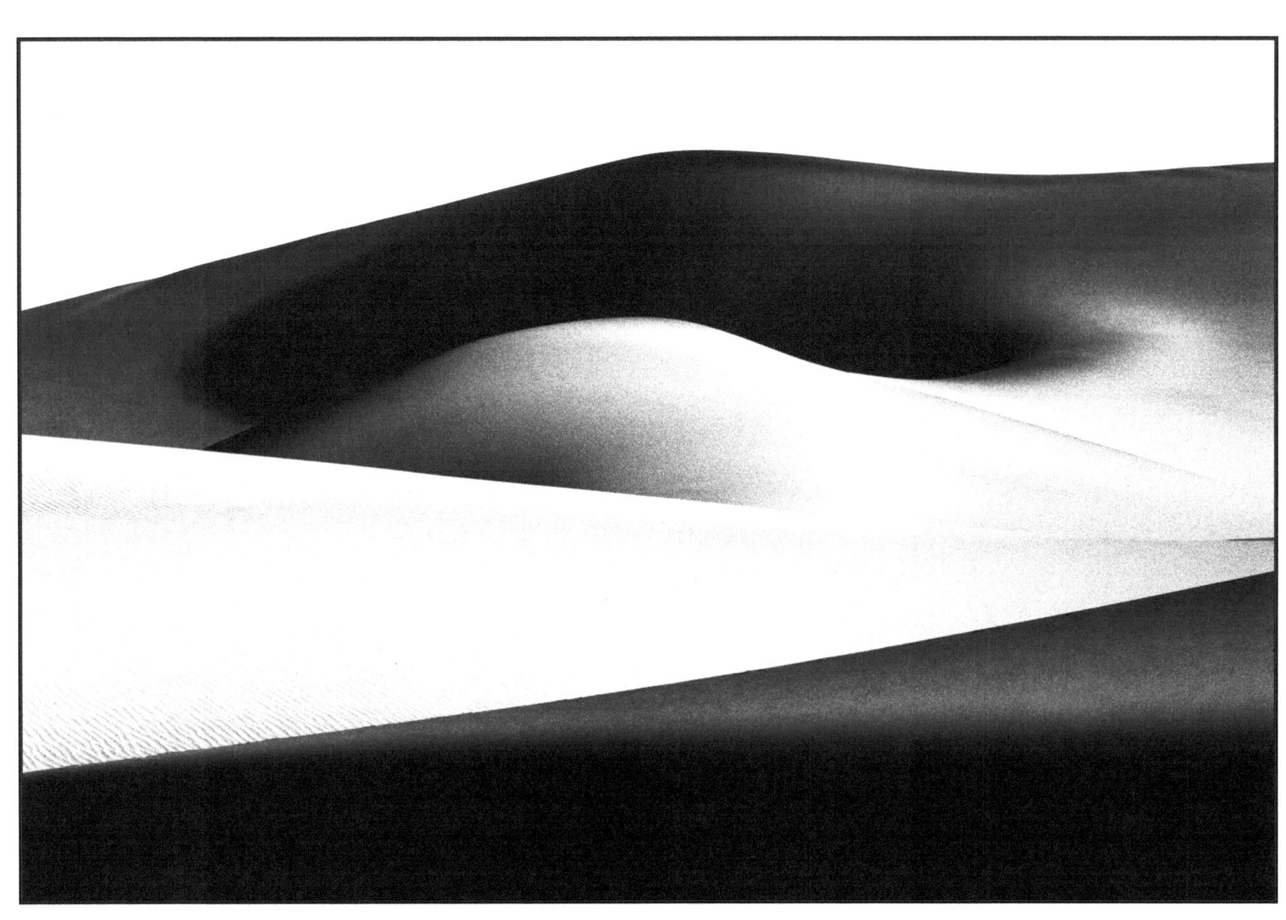

Eureka Valley Sand Dunes - Death Valley National Park, California 1996

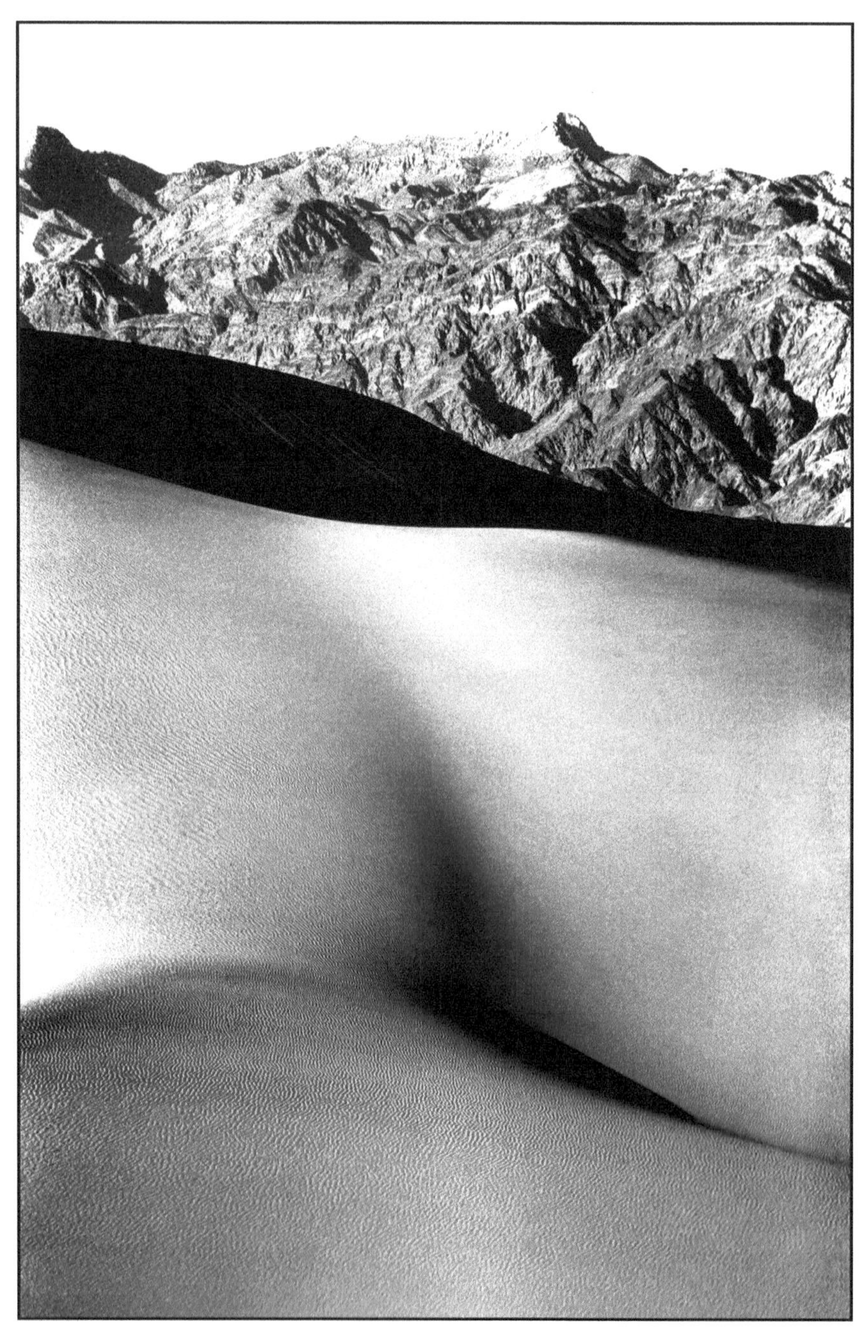

Mesquite Flat Dunes - Death Valley National Park, California 1996

Mesquite Flat Dunes - Death Valley National Park, California 1996

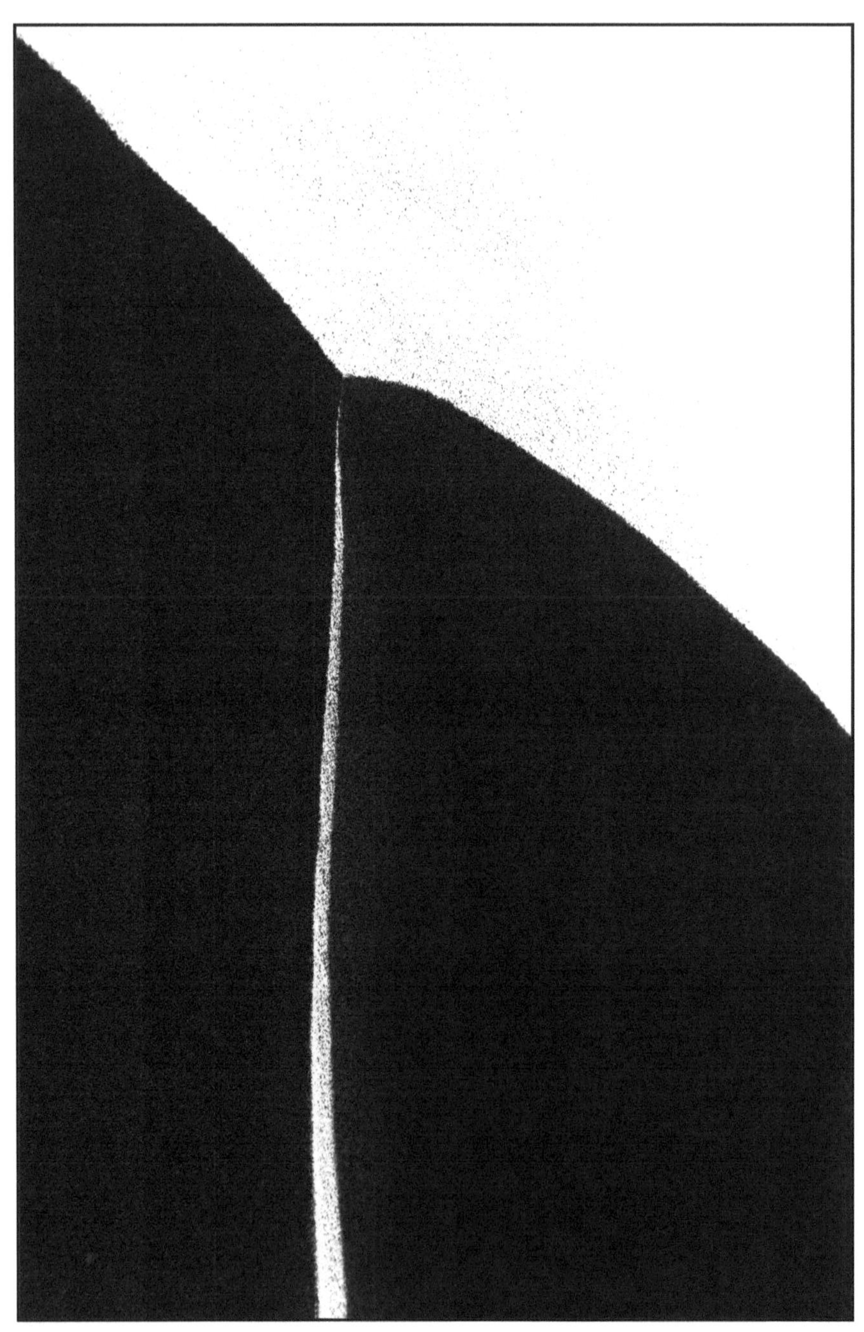

 Mesquite Flat Dunes - Death Valley National Park, California 1994

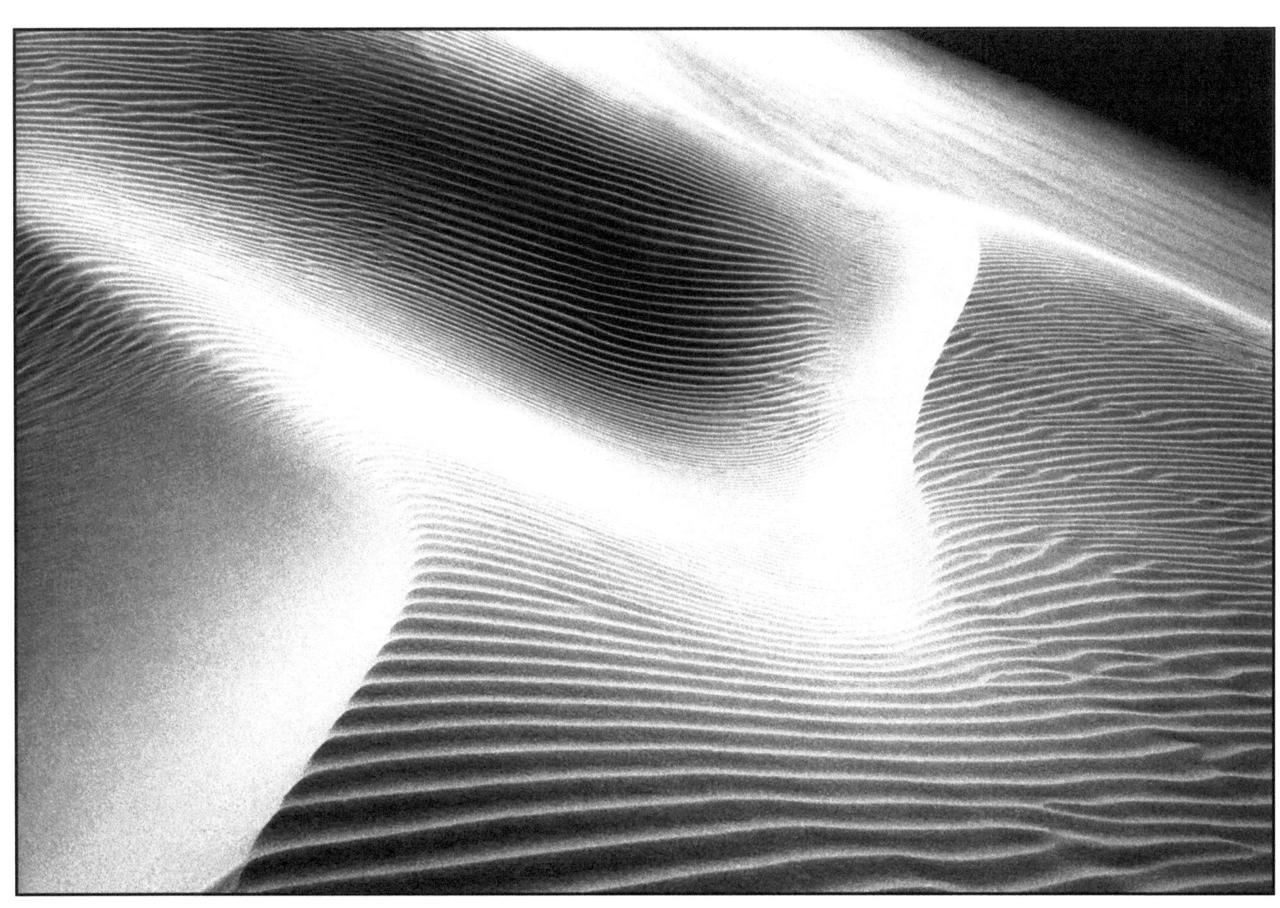

Mesquite Flat Dunes - Death Valley National Park, California 1994

Acknowledgements

Thanks to:

Anita Pinedo Touchet for pointing me in the direction of the Dunes of Coro in Venezeula where she grew up.

Sebastian Piras who first displayed these photos in the restaurant he managed on West Broadway in SOHO (New York City)

Lynne Holton who accompanied me while I was photographing many of the dunes.

Photographer Bio

BOOKS: R*EJOICE WHEN YOU DIE* - The New Orleans Jazz Funerals
DUET - Peot & Photographer - Elizabeth Burk & Leo Touchet
PEOPLE AMONG US - Photography by Leo Touchet
AT THE RACES - Photography by Leo Touchet
FLOWERS - In Black & White

COLLECTIONS: Sir Elton John Photography Collection, New Orelans Museum of Art, Houston Museum of Fine Arts, Bibliotheque National (France), Everson Museum of Art, Schomburg Center (New York Public Library), Chase Manhattan Collection, U.S. National Park Service.

PUBLICATIONS: Life Magazine, Time Magazine, Time Life Books, National Geographic Books, Newsweek Magazine, Fortune Magazine, Natural History Magazine, New York Times, Washington Post, Boston Globe, Oxford American Magazine, Southern Quarterly, Southern Living Magazine, America Illustrated (USIA), Der Stern (Germany), Panorama (Italy), Popular Photography.

EXHIBITIONS: Acadiana Center for the Arts, Arizona State University, Arkansas Art Center, Brooks Memorial (Memphis), Columbus Musuem (Georgia), Everson Museum (Syracuse), Fotofest '92 (Houston), Hofstra University (New York), Louisiana State University, Miami Art Center, Mint Museum (North Carolina), Mississippi Southern University, New Orleans Public Library, Oklahoma Art Center, Public Theater (New York City), Royal Ontario Museum (Toronto), University of Houston, University of Oklahoma, University of Texas.

GROUP EXHIBITIONS:
*REGARDS et MEMOIRES - ARLES 2008 - 39*th Annual Arles, France Photo Expo
(Four Exhibitions including Public Street Banners on the rue de la Roquette)
PHOTOGRAPHY USA 1976, United States Bicentennial Exhibition
(USIA exhibition circulated in the Soviet Union and East Europe).

Leo Touchet's Website: **www.leotouchet.com**

For print sales: Contact Coco Conroy **coco@jacksonfineart.com**Jackson Fine Art Gallery in Atlanta, Georgia

Other Photo Books by
LEO TOUCHET

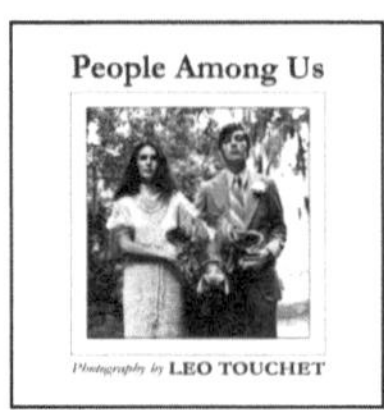

People Among Us - *Photography by Leo Touchet*

ISBN: 9781732443303 - 8.5 x 8.5 inches - 46 Pages - Paperback
Black & white photographs of people around the world.

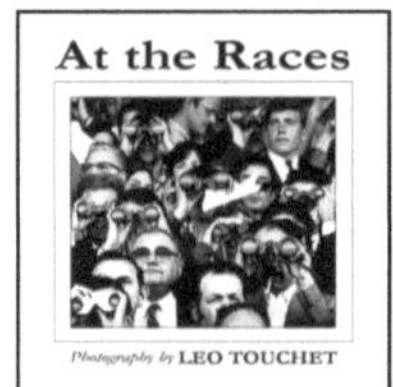

At The Races - *Photography by Leo Touchet*

ISBN: 9781732443310 - 8.5 x 8.5 inches - 42 Pages - Paperback
Black & white photographs of people at horse race tracks.

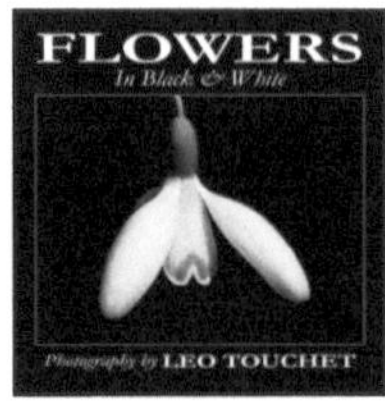

Flowers - *In Black & White*

ISBN: 9781732443334 - 8.5 x 8.5 inches - 36 Pages - Paperback
Black & white photographs of flowers.

These books are available from:
www.photocirclepress.com

www.ingramcontent.com/pod-product-compliance
Lightning Source LLC
LaVergne TN
LVHW070159110826
845147LV00002B/450

* 9 7 8 1 7 3 2 4 4 3 3 2 7 *